W9-CGM-969

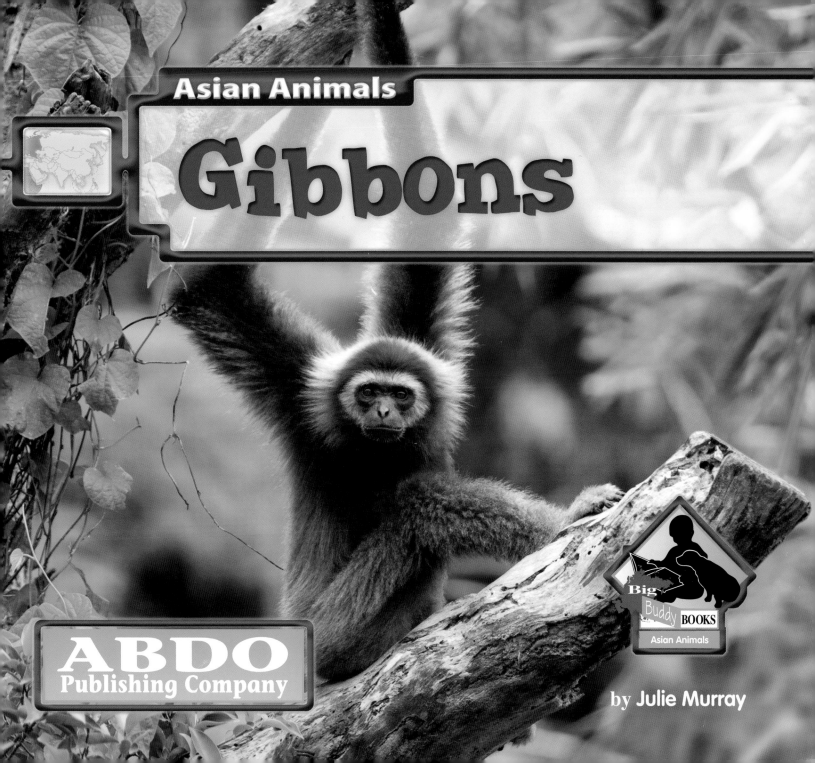

Gibbons

ABDO
Publishing Company

Big Buddy BOOKS
Asian Animals

by Julie Murray

VISIT US AT
www.abdopublishing.com

Published by ABDO Publishing Company, PO Box 398166, Minneapolis, Minnesota 55439.

Copyright © 2013 by Abdo Consulting Group, Inc. International copyrights reserved in all countries. No part of this book may be reproduced in any form without written permission from the publisher. Big Buddy Books™ is a trademark and logo of ABDO Publishing Company.

Printed in the United States of America, North Mankato, Minnesota.
102012
012013

 PRINTED ON RECYCLED PAPER

Coordinating Series Editor: Rochelle Baltzer
Editor: Marcia Zappa
Contributing Editors: Megan M. Gunderson, Sarah Tieck
Graphic Design: Maria Hosley
Cover Photograph: *Shutterstock*: Kjersti Joergensen.
Interior Photographs/Illustrations: *Animals Animals-Earth Scenes*: Odell, Lynn P. (p. 19), Robinson, William (p. 27); *Getty Images*: Ingo Arndt (p. 25), Gerry Ellis/Minden Pictures (p. 25), JOERG KOCH/AFP (p. 27), David Maitland (p. 17), Visuals Unlimited, Inc./Thomas Marent (pp. 7, 29), Marvin E. Newman (p. 23), Joe Petersburger/National Geographic (p. 21), Anna Yu (p. 15); *Glow Images*: Arco Images GmbH Wegner, P. (p. 11), Gerard Lacz/Anka Agency (pp. 5, 15), J & C Sohns/PicturePress (p. 13), Juergen & Christine Sohns/PicturePress (p. 13); *iStockphoto*: ©iStockphoto.com/HU-JUN (p. 4), ©iStockphoto.com/DavorLovincic (p. 9); *Shutterstock*: Image Focus (p. 4) Peerakit Jirachetthakun POPCITY (p. 9), LiteChoices (p. 8) Igor Prahin (p. 9), Worakit Sirijinda (p. 17).

Library of Congress Cataloging-in-Publication Data

Murray, Julie, 1969-
  Gibbons / Julie Murray.
    p. cm. -- (Asian animals)
  Audience: 7-11
  ISBN 978-1-61783-554-4
  1. Gibbons--Asia--Juvenile literature. I. Title.
  QL737.P96M8732 2013
  599.88'2--dc23
                              2012030979

Contents

Long ago, nearly all land on Earth was one big mass. About 200 million years ago, the land began to break into **continents**. One of these continents is Asia.

Gibbons are a type of small ape. They are known for swinging through treetops.

Asia is the largest **continent**. It includes many countries and **cultures**. It also has different types of land and interesting animals. One of these animals is the gibbon. In the wild, gibbons are only found in Asia.

Gibbon Territory

There are more than ten different types of gibbons. Most live in areas of South and Southeast Asia.

Gibbons live in thick forests. These forests are usually warm and wet.

Gibbon Territory

Gibbons spend almost their whole lives in trees.

Welcome to Asia!

If you took a trip to where gibbons live, you might find…

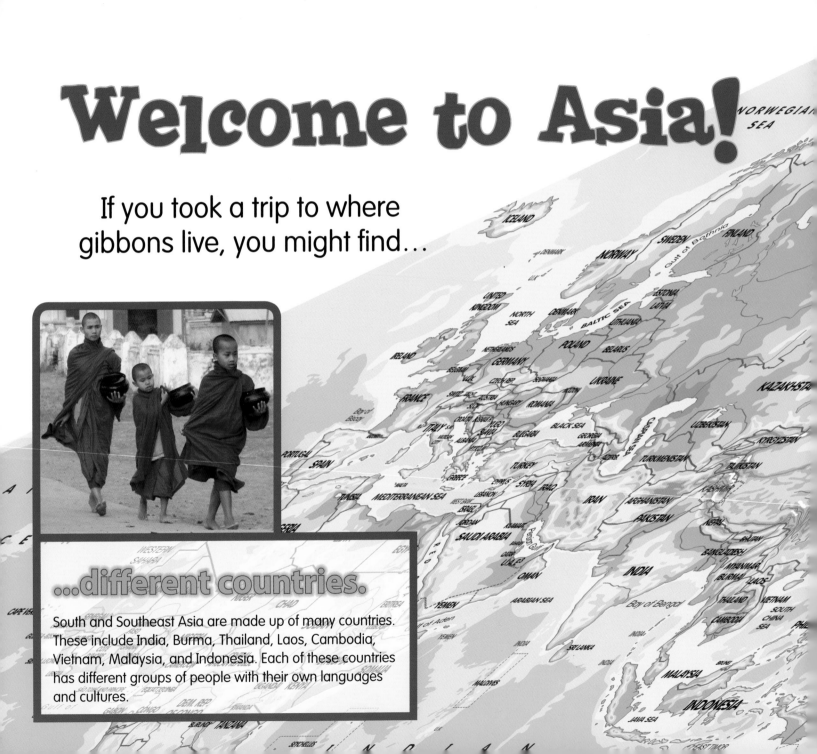

…different countries.

South and Southeast Asia are made up of many countries. These include India, Burma, Thailand, Laos, Cambodia, Vietnam, Malaysia, and Indonesia. Each of these countries has different groups of people with their own languages and cultures.

...small villages and big cities.

Most people in South and Southeast Asia live in small villages. Still, almost all of the countries in South and Southeast Asia have at least one big city. These include Jakarta in Indonesia and Bangkok (*left*) in Thailand.

...islands.

Southeast Asia includes thousands of islands. Gibbons live on many of them, including Borneo, Sumatra (*right*), and Java.

...rice.

Rice is a common crop in South and Southeast Asia. And, it is an important food. Many people there eat rice with every meal! It is often served with seafood or vegetables.

9

Take a Closer Look

Gibbons are small, thin animals. Their bodies and legs are short compared to their long arms. Gibbons do not have tails. Adult gibbons stand 15 to 36 inches (38 to 91 cm) tall. They weigh 9 to 29 pounds (4 to 13 kg). Most males and females are close to the same size.

Uncovered!

Gibbons are called lesser apes because of their small size. They are closely related to the great apes, which include bonobos, chimpanzees, gorillas, and orangutans.

The largest type of gibbon is called the siamang (SEE-uh-mang).

A gibbon's head is small and round. Its face has two dark eyes, a small nose, and a thin mouth.

Gibbons have soft, thick fur. It can be many colors including tan, brown, gray, or black. Different types of gibbons are often recognized by their fur color. And, females are usually lighter colors than males.

Skin covers a gibbon's face, its armpits, and the bottoms of its hands and feet. And, a gibbon has firm pads of skin on its rear.

White-handed gibbons have white fur on their hands and feet. Darker fur covers their bodies.

Black-crested gibbons have a strip of extra-long, black fur on top of their heads.

13

Swinging Away

Living high in treetops makes it easy for gibbons to find food. And, it keeps them safe from many predators.

Gibbons move through treetops by swinging from branch to branch. This type of movement is called brachiating (BRAY-kee-ay-tihng).

Other times, gibbons walk on two legs. They do this up high on tree branches and sometimes on the ground. When gibbons walk, they hold up their arms for balance.

Gibbons can swing through treetops as fast as 35 miles (56 km) per hour!

15

Gibbons are well built for swinging through treetops. Their long, strong arms easily hold up their light bodies. They also allow them to reach faraway branches. Gibbons use their long, curved hands like hooks to hold on to branches.

The skin on a gibbon's hands and feet help it hold on to branches.

A gibbon's shoulders and wrists can bend easily. This allows a gibbon to swing fast through treetops.

Family Life

Gibbons live in small family groups. A family usually includes adult male and female **mates** and their young.

Each gibbon family has its own home area. It does not allow other gibbons to enter this space. Family members warn others to stay away by singing loud, long songs.

A gibbon chooses one mate for its whole life. This is unusual for apes.

Uncovered!

Gibbons chase or scare away strangers from their family's home area. They swing or leap wildly and break branches. They almost never fight.

19

Gibbons spend their days with their family. They eat and sing together. They also **groom** each other.

At night, gibbons sleep near their family members. They do not build nests like other apes. But, they often sleep tucked into the forks of trees.

Uncovered!
Because they live high in trees, gibbons have few natural predators. Their predators include leopards and large snakes and birds.

Gibbons sleep sitting up with their arms wrapped around their legs.

Sweet Songs

Gibbons are known for the songs they sing to guard their home areas. These songs are long and complex. Male and female mates often sing together. Sometimes, their young join in.

A gibbon's songs are loud. They can be heard up to one mile (1.6 km) away. Siamang gibbons have extra-loud songs. They have large pouches of skin under their chins that fill with air. This helps their songs carry up to two miles (3.2 km) away!

Uncovered!
A female gibbon's songs are different from a male's. Usually, a female has louder, more recognizable calls.

Gibbons are often considered the most musical land mammals. Many people believe their songs are very beautiful.

23

Uncovered!
Gibbons find the water they need in treetops. Often, they dip their hands into puddles of water or rub them on wet leaves. Then, they suck the water off their fur.

Mealtime

Gibbons eat many different foods found in their treetop homes. About two-thirds of what they eat is fruit, such as figs. Gibbons also eat leaves, flowers, and bark. And sometimes, they eat bugs, eggs, and small animals.

Like humans, gibbons have opposable thumbs that move freely of their other fingers. This makes it easy for them to hold things. Gibbons also have opposable big toes. So, they can hold things with their feet!

Gibbons can reach food far out on tree branches that other animals cannot.

25

Baby Gibbons

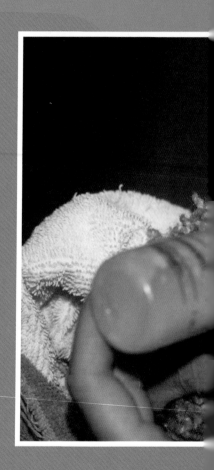

Gibbons are mammals. Females usually have one baby at a time. At birth, a gibbon baby weighs less than 21.5 ounces (610 g). It drinks its mother's milk and grows.

At first, a baby gibbon clings to its mother's belly. Later, it begins to follow her through the treetops. After about a year, a young gibbon stops drinking milk. It stays with its family for six to ten years. Then, it is ready to start a family of its own.

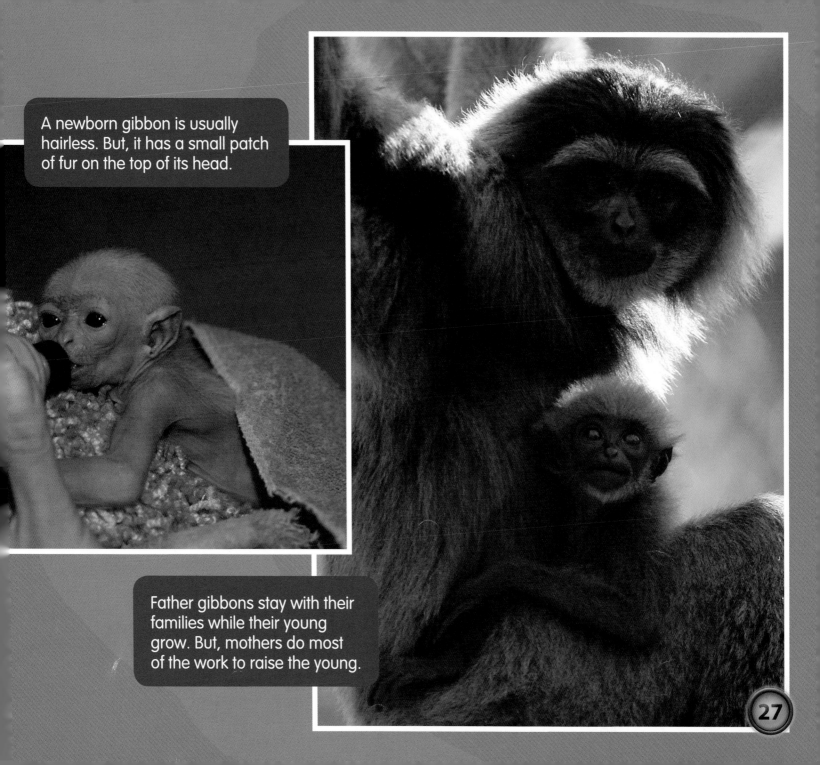

A newborn gibbon is usually hairless. But, it has a small patch of fur on the top of its head.

Father gibbons stay with their families while their young grow. But, mothers do most of the work to raise the young.

Survivors

Life in Asia isn't easy for gibbons. New buildings and farms take over their **habitats**. People kill them for their meat and to use their body parts in **medicine**. And, people capture young gibbons to sell as pets.

Still, gibbons **survive**. There are laws against killing them. But, more needs to be done to make sure these animals continue to live freely. Gibbons help make Asia an amazing place!

In the wild, gibbons live for 25 to 40 years.

Uncovered!

Most types of gibbons are endangered. This means they are in great danger of dying out. A few types of gibbons are critically endangered. This means they are in even greater danger of dying out.

Wow!
I'll bet you never knew...

...that gibbons are great leapers. They can reach faraway trees by taking huge, swinging leaps. In this way, gibbons can cross gaps of 30 feet (9 m) or more!

...that gibbons from the same area have similar songs. Scientists can often recognize the type of gibbon and where it is from based on its songs.

...that gibbons cannot swim. They stay away from bodies of water. In fact, large rivers separate different types of gibbons.

Important Words

complex having many parts, often related in a difficult way.

continent one of Earth's seven main land areas.

culture (KUHL-chuhr) the arts, beliefs, and ways of life of a group of people.

groom to clean and care for.

habitat a place where a living thing is naturally found.

mammal a member of a group of living beings. Mammals make milk to feed their babies and usually have hair or fur on their skin.

mates members of a couple joined together in order to reproduce, or have babies.

medicine (MEH-duh-suhn) an item used in or on the body to treat an illness, ease pain, or heal a wound.

survive to continue to live or exist.

Web Sites

To learn more about gibbons, visit ABDO Publishing Company online. Web sites about gibbons are featured on our Book Links page. These links are routinely monitored and updated to provide the most current information available.

www.abdopublishing.com

Index